D1203473

Coding

Cover: A user works on a coding tutorial using a tablet computer.

Norwood House Press
P.O. Box 316598
Chicago, Illinois 60631

For information regarding Norwood House Press, please visit our website at:
www.norwoodhousepress.com or call 866-565-2900.

PHOTO CREDITS: Cover: © Marcio Jose Sanchez/AP Images; © Belyaevskiy/iStockphoto, 19; © da-kuk/iStockphoto, 37; © Everett Collection, 29; © fstop123/iStockphoto, 5, 13; © Jeff Chiu/AP Images, 30; © mariusFM77 /iStockphoto, 14; © Mark Lennihan/AP Images, 32; © martin-dm/iStockphoto, 24; © Matthew Corley/Shutterstock Images, 38; © mikkelwilliam/iStockphoto, 11; © National Physical Laboratory/Crown Copyright/Science Source, 9; © Paul Sakuma/AP Images, 21; © Rex Features/AP Images, 39; © Seth Wenig/AP Images, 41; © Toria/Shutterstock Images, 12; © vgajic/iStockphoto, 35; © Wachiwit/iStockphoto, 26; © Yuri_ Arcurs/iStockphoto, 16

Hardcover ISBN: 978-1-59953-887-7
Paperback ISBN: 978-1-68404-118-3

© 2018 by Norwood House Press.

LIBRARY OF CONGRESS CATALOGING-IN-PUBLICATION DATA

Names: Marquardt, Meg, author.
Title: Coding / by Meg Marquardt.
Description: Chicago, Illinois : Norwood House Press, 2017. | Series: Tech
   bytes | Audience: Ages 8-12. | Audience: Grades 4 to 6. | Includes
   bibliographical references and index.
Identifiers: LCCN 2017002713 (print) | LCCN 2017003619 (ebook) | ISBN
   9781599538877 (library edition : alk. paper) | ISBN 9781684041237 (eBook)
Subjects: LCSH: Computer programming--Juvenile literature.
Classification: LCC QA76.52 .M374 2017 (print) | LCC QA76.52 (ebook) | DDC
   005.1--dc23
LC record available at https://lccn.loc.gov/2017002713

302N—072017
Manufactured in the United States of America in North Mankato, Minnesota.

CONTENTS

Chapter 1:
A World of Computers   4

Chapter 2:
What Is Code?   14

Chapter 3:
Coding in the Real World   22

Chapter 4:
Coding for Tomorrow   31

Glossary   43

For More Information   44

Index   46

About the Author   48

Note: Words that are **bolded** in the text are defined in the glossary.

A World of Computers

For hundreds of years, machines have made life easier for people. In the 1800s, trains made it easier to move cargo and passengers over long distances. In the 1900s, home appliances made it easier to store and prepare food. Today, the machine that makes the biggest difference in people's everyday lives is the computer.

Computers make a wide assortment of tasks easier. People use them to send and receive messages, pictures, and videos. Students use them to write papers, and workers use them to create budgets. Computers are used for relaxation, too. People watch movies and play games on them. One of the most useful things about computers is that they can be used for so many tasks. This flexibility comes from programs and coding.

A program is a set of instructions that a computer carries out. Some programs let users create documents or spreadsheets. Other programs play movies or music. Some are thrilling video games. Coding is the process of writing the instructions that

Computers and tablets are now found in most US schools and homes.

make up these programs. By dreaming up new types of programs, coders expand the potential of computers.

Computers cannot understand instructions written in plain English. Coders must learn to write programs in

What Does Code Look Like?

Every coding language looks slightly different. Many use symbols and special acronyms. Often, programming instructions may be tough to read for an untrained coder. Here is an example from the Java programming language. This code writes the words "Hello World!" on the screen. Writing a "Hello World" program is a common first step for coders studying a new programming language.

```
public class HelloWorld
{
    public static void
main(String[] args) {
        System.out.
println("Hello World!");
    }
}
```

a way that a computer can understand. Coders write in a variety of different programming languages. These languages use different sets of words, numbers, and symbols to make up their instructions. Hundreds of programming languages are in use today.

Modern computers have been around for only a few decades, but the idea of programming languages has a long history. One of the first people to think about coding was the pioneering Ada Lovelace. She carried out her work in the early 1800s.

Creating the First Code

Lovelace was born in 1815. She had a nontraditional upbringing. Unlike most girls of her time, she was encouraged to learn math and science. During her studies, she met scientist Charles Babbage. Babbage had designed a mechanical device that could be used for mathematics.

Babbage's machine was known as the Difference Engine. It was much different from today's computers. Rather than electricity, circuits, and microchips, it would use levers and gears. It could quickly carry out math problems that would take a person hours to calculate by hand. The user would set the device to the initial settings for the problem, then turn a crank to put the machine into motion.

DID YOU KNOW?

Ada Lovelace was the daughter of Lord Byron, a famous British poet. Byron left the family when Ada was a child. Her mother worried Ada would become moody and unpredictable like her father. She felt that having Ada focus on studying math and science would prevent this.

However, the full machine was not built during Babbage's lifetime.

Babbage also envisioned a machine that could do even more complicated math. He called it the Analytical Engine. Ada Lovelace was fascinated by the project. She worked on translating articles about Babbage's machines written by engineers and scientists. One was written by Italian engineer Luigi Federico Menabrea. As Lovelace translated it to English, she added her own notes about the machine. The original article was around 8,000 words long. Lovelace's translation and notes came out to over 20,000 words.

Her notes suggested that the machine could do much more than complex math problems. She imagined a machine that could be taught that numbers stood for other things. She thought of a machine that could make music. For example, the machine would know that a certain string of numbers was an instruction to play a particular note. She was a pioneer in thinking about how computers could be used for different tasks by giving them different instructions.

Building More Complex Machines

Since Lovelace's day, computers and coding have come a long way. In the 1940s, German inventor Konrad Zuse created what is considered the first modern computer. Called the Z3, it could remember and carry out instructions.

US programming pioneer Grace Hopper worked with early computers during World War II. She later helped in the development of the UNIVAC I computer and a programming language called COBOL. Hopper served in the US Naval Reserve, helping the US Navy develop and use early computers. She eventually rose to the rank of rear admiral.

Ada Lovelace is often considered the first computer programmer.

Scientists and engineers continued to build improved computers. By the 1950s, there was an explosion of coding languages. Computer company IBM released FORTRAN in 1957. Updated versions of this language are still in use today. In the 1960s, programming grew beyond solving mathematical problems. Computers became powerful enough for coders to make drawings or animation. These early roots eventually led to modern computer-animated movies.

In the 1970s and 1980s, personal computers became widely available. Millions of people now had computers in their homes. Programming was no longer only for experts in labs or universities. People could learn to create their own games or other programs.

The 1990s brought the Internet, changing the world of computers forever. The Internet is a framework connecting computers around the world. Data travels from one computer to another across this vast network. One of the major uses

The First Home Computers

The companies Apple and IBM made early personal computers. Some ads showed the computers as being useful in the kitchen. Users could store recipes and create meal plans with them. Other ads showed how useful computers could be for home budgets. These early computers were not as easy to use as today's machines. The user often needed to have programming knowledge to use them. Today, most users never see the code behind the programs they use. All these instructions are carried out behind the scenes.

Early personal computers were much bulkier than the ones used today.

The Internet connects computer users all over the world.

of the Internet is the World Wide Web. It is a set of interconnected pages that Internet users can access online. Another use for the Internet is e-mail, a system for sending and receiving messages. Using the Internet, coders could now share programs with other users. They could also write programs for the World Wide Web.

Smartphones and tablets changed the programming landscape in the 2000s. Programs, also known as apps, turned these devices into powerful tools for both work and fun. And new programming tools made coding accessible to more people than ever before.

Today, the future of programming is bright. Computers, smartphones, and tablets can be found in practically every part of society. These machines make modern life more efficient and fun. Inventive coders will continue to make new advances, creating innovative programs that unlock the potential of our computerized world.

Some smartphone apps let users listen to music.

CHAPTER 2

What Is Code?

When using a computer, a person interacts with two related things: hardware and software. The computer's hardware is made up of its physical parts. The screen, keyboard, and mouse are all hardware. The parts inside the computer, such as the **processor** and memory, are also hardware.

The computer's software is made up of all the programs it runs. Some programs manage how the hardware and software

Web browsers allow users to access social media, videos, search engines, and more.

work together. These are called **operating systems**. Other programs include word processors, **web browsers**, and games.

Each programming language has its own strengths and weaknesses, and each is best for different kinds of programs. Some work well for making video games, while others are better suited for simple programs on desktop computers. A few of today's major languages include C#, Python, Java, and Swift.

Regardless of the language, all code has the same basic function. Code is a list of instructions for the computer processor to follow. Processors can handle instructions only in **binary**—long sequences of ones and zeroes. The most basic programming language, machine code, consists of only ones and zeroes. Binary instructions can

be extremely difficult for coders to write and read. To make programming easier, people have developed programming languages that use symbols, letters, and words. Before these instructions go to

the processor, they are converted into the equivalent series of ones and zeroes.

Finding Errors

Programmers use **compiler** software to convert a program into binary. They feed in the code they wrote, and the compiler spits out the ones and zeroes that a processor can understand. Compiler software also helps programmers find errors in their code. If something is mistyped or formatted incorrectly, a compiler can often catch the problem. This is known as a syntax error. A piece of software may have thousands of lines of code, so it is not unusual for errors to appear.

Errors in code look different than typos in regular text. The language C# uses symbols such as %, {, &, and *. These symbols can tell a program to go look in a specific area to find information. Accidentally leaving out a single * could bring a program to a sudden halt. When a programmer tries to run software and it doesn't work at all, he or she knows a syntax error may be lurking somewhere in the code.

Another type of programming error is called a runtime error. This is a problem that occurs while a program is running. The program may seem to run normally at first, but some of its features might not be working correctly. Problems like these are also known as bugs.

Dealing with Bugs

The use of the term *bug* to describe general errors predates computers. One of its early uses in computer errors came from an incident in September 1947. Technicians were working on a US military computer. At that time, computers were the size of entire rooms. Something went wrong with the computer, and the workers searched for the problem. They found that a moth had gotten stuck in one of its parts and caused the issue. Computer pioneer Grace Hopper wrote in the log book, "First actual case of bug being found."

In computers, a bug can cause a game to crash. It may cause a music app to suddenly skip songs. It might make a video chat suddenly disconnect. But some bugs can be much more serious. One of these happened on September 23, 1983.

On that date, alarm bells sounded in a Russian military base. The base's software said that the United States had just launched nuclear missiles at Russia. Commanders thought they might need to fire their own missiles. This would result in a devastating war. But Lieutenant Colonel Stanislaus Petrov did not think the missiles were really coming. It turned out a software bug had made the alarms sound. A software error could have led to a war. Instead, Petrov was able to guess that something wasn't quite right.

Living in a world of computers means knowing that sometimes software will not work as intended. There will be errors and mistakes in the code. In a process called debugging, coders find and fix these errors to make their software work better.

Thinking Like a Programmer

Programming is not just a job. It is also a mindset. Thinking like a programmer makes it easier to code successfully.

There are many aspects to thinking like a programmer. First, programmers should keep in mind that they are writing code that computers need to understand. Unless there is a flaw in the hardware,

HTML

One of the most common ways of writing things on the World Wide Web involves the HyperText Markup Language (HTML). At first HTML may look like code, but it actually just describes how a website will look. HTML gives web browsers instructions on the size, typeface, arrangement, and formatting of text and pictures online. Though HTML isn't a programming language, it works together with programming languages to make exciting websites. A programming language called JavaScript is used to make websites more interactive. JavaScript is different from the similarly named Java programming language. JavaScript code is sometimes added directly into the HTML text that makes up a website.

HTML is the language that makes up most websites.

computers don't make mistakes. They do exactly what their instructions say. Errors in these instructions are the source of problems. Programmers must logically think about how the computer will interpret their instructions to prevent such issues.

DID YOU KNOW?

Each year, the National STEM Video Game Challenge encourages students to program their own video games. In 2016, nearly 5,000 students entered the challenge. The games did not have to be about science. The goal was for students to use science and technology skills to code creative and fun games.

coding project can seem overwhelming. It may be for an app or game that has many features. Thinking about logical ways to split up the project can make the coding process go more smoothly. It also makes it easier to share the work with other programmers.

This is another part of thinking like a programmer: collaborating with others. Programmers often work on projects in teams. They must try to write their code as clearly as possible so that their fellow coders can understand it. Programmers collaborate online, too. Websites such as Stack Overflow give them a place to ask and answer coding questions. The website GitHub allows programmers to share their code with others. Users of these sites must be at least 13 years old.

Another part of thinking like a programmer is breaking up big problems into more manageable pieces. A major

Linus Torvalds

When most people get a new computer, they use whatever operating system the computer comes with. Today's most common operating systems are Windows and macOS. Another popular operating system, Linux, dates back to 1991. In that year, a Finnish student named Linus Torvalds decided he could make his own operating system. It soon became known as Linux. Torvalds made it free to use. Torvalds' major innovation was that it was easy for other coders to make changes to Linux. These changes are shared online. Over time, the development of Linux split into several different branches. Different groups of coders took the operating system in different directions. These different versions of Linux are known as distributions. Major distributions used today include Fedora and Ubuntu.

Torvalds with the mascot of Linux, a penguin

Thinking like a programmer is useful for more than just coders. Thinking logically, splitting up problems, and collaborating with others are good things for anyone to do when working on any sort of daily task.

CHAPTER 3

Coding in the Real World

Coding is literally all around us. Because most of the world runs on computers, coding is an important part of keeping information safe and secure. But criminals, sometimes called hackers, can use their coding skills to break the law. Coding skills are also valuable at major businesses for keeping track of vast amounts of data. At the same time, code plays a role in entertaining people, making amazing special effects possible.

Encryption

Security is a major issue online. People may send e-mails about sensitive information. They may look up personal health-care data or access their bank accounts. If these systems were not secure, someone may be able to steal data or even money. Luckily, coders have developed **encryption** programs to help keep information safe online.

Encryption software works by obscuring the true contents of messages

Apps that Save Lives

Part of being a programmer is thinking of how real-world problems can be solved using code. Some of these problems are simple. For example, a person who needs to keep a budget may develop a budgeting program. Other types of programs may be designed to save lives. One such app has information on how to survive a natural disaster. Another has a host of first aid information in case of an emergency. Many apps are also designed for use by doctors, especially in rural areas. Some apps can be used to help with the diagnosis of a disease. For example, an app was developed to identify instances of milky eyes in pictures. This can be a sign of a type of eye cancer. By always looking out for problems in the world, programmers can create software that helps people live safer and healthier lives.

sent online. For instance, a program might turn each letter in a message into another letter. Every *A* may become a *B*, and every *N* may become a *Q*. The word *an* would appear as *bq* instead. The person receiving the message would have software that knows which letters are which. The message would be unscrambled. But if a person intercepted the message, they would see only the unreadable encrypted message.

Programmers who work on encryption software have to adapt to new situations. Criminals or spies may attempt to break encryption systems. If they succeed, they can read the encrypted text, which

to let users get access to information they aren't supposed to see. Other programs are designed to annoy users or even steal money. These are known as malware. One major type of malware is known as a virus.

Viruses are pieces of code that are typically hidden inside another file. For example, a programmer may add virus code to a music file. When a person downloads that file and plays the song, the computer also carries out the instructions in the virus's code. Once on the computer, viruses can wreak havoc. They may delete files or steal information. They may

may include passwords, bank account numbers, and sensitive information. Encryption software has to be on the cutting edge at all times to keep data safe.

Hacking

Not all programmers have good intentions. Some programs are specifically designed prevent a computer from being used until the user pays the hacker money. They may even allow the hacker to control the computer. Companies create antivirus software to find and delete viruses from computers. A constant struggle exists between hackers and antivirus coders.

Big Data

In recent years, computer programmers have been dealing with the phenomenon known as big data. Social networks, businesses, schools, scientists, and others are collecting huge amounts of data all the time. Programmers have learned how to manage all that information and make it useful.

One of the biggest sets of data on the planet is owned by Facebook. The social

DID YOU KNOW?

One of the first-ever hacks was in 1903. Guglielmo Marconi, inventor of the telegraph, had set up a demonstration to show how secure telegraph messages were. However, another scientist intercepted the messages. That scientist sent ridiculous messages to the public demonstration instead.

networking website, which began in 2004, had approximately 1.8 billion users by 2016. These users share photos, talk

Social media apps often store huge amounts of data about their users.

with friends, and fill their profile pages with the celebrities and brands they like most. Facebook uses all this data to help advertisers target users' specific interests. The company also collects information about how people use Facebook, even recording how long users hold the mouse over certain parts of the page. It uses this kind of information when redesigning how the website looks.

Making Movies with Code

Computers and programming have revolutionized the movie industry. This revolution is clear in today's incredible special effects. Programmers in this field are often artists and designers, too. Computer-generated special effects first came to film in the 1970s. One of the first major milestones was the 1973 movie *Westworld*. In that movie, artists worked with programmers to create a scene from the point of view of a robot. The robot could sense body heat. Programmers made a short sequence where the whole screen is red, except a patch of yellow and orange where a human is standing.

Another major milestone was **three-dimensional** computer graphics. Programmers faced a big challenge when it came to making a virtual creature in a movie look lifelike next to real people. The 1993 movie *Jurassic Park* was the first movie to show off this new skill. Artists drew and sculpted dinosaurs in different poses. This work was scanned into a computer. Coders used animation software to make the dinosaur models

move. Other artists created skin textures to make the dinosaurs look lifelike. All of these elements came together to create a dinosaur that could be placed into a scene.

Some movies are completely computer generated. Companies such as Pixar and DreamWorks create animated movies solely on computers. They use software created especially for the task. Programmers who make this animation software find ways to make things move in realistic ways. They also figure out how to make light and shadows look realistic in a scene. In the world of movies, artists and programmers work together to make beautiful films.

Gaming

Programming is a central part of the video game industry. In some ways, programming video games is similar to the work programmers do for movies. Both fields often involve creating virtual

Each step required complex programming to make sure all the pieces fit together.

objects, then animating and lighting them in realistic ways. But unlike movies, video games are interactive. When a player presses a button on the controller, something happens on screen. This interactivity means that there are many ways a scene in a video game could play out. As a result, video games are full of very complex code to handle all these situations. In addition to animation and lighting, code controls the physics of the game world. If a character throws an object, the physics code determines how far the object goes and what happens when it hits something else.

Code Is Everywhere

Whether it is used for a top-secret security system, a major company's

The 1995 film *Toy Story* broke new ground for computer animation.

Code Bootcamps

With so many coding jobs, the need for talented programmers is growing. Though a person can get a college degree in programming, other educational pathways have become available. One such method is a coding bootcamp. Bootcamps are intense, immersive classes in programming. Some are only nine weeks long. They usually focus on the specific kind of programming needed for a job. For example, if a person is looking for a job writing mobile apps, a bootcamp will focus on app programming. Bootcamps are becoming particularly popular among young people, as well as in developing countries. In places where unemployment is high, this style of training can be a quick way to find a new career.

A teacher works with a student at a code bootcamp.

data research, or an entertaining movie or video game, code is a major part of our world. Learning how code works is critical to understanding how computers have changed modern life. The flexibility of programming means that computers can tackle just about any task coders can dream up.

CHAPTER 4

Coding for Tomorrow

Students learn to read and write in school. But what if they learned to code, too? Many schools are beginning to teach coding in the classroom. And students of all ages can use online tools to start learning programming in their free time. As computers continue to reach into almost every part of daily life, learning about code is becoming more important. Even if a student does not want to become a programmer, knowing how code works will help them understand the world in which he or she lives.

Hour of Code

In 2013, an organization called Code.org was formed. Its goal is to bring coding to as many people as possible. The group particularly targets students who may not otherwise have access to computer science education. Many of their events are focused on recruiting girls and people of color. Because coding is such an important part of the digital world, it is important to make sure everyone has an equal opportunity to learn about it.

Code.org is home to Hour of Code. This 60-minute program is designed to introduce students of all ages to coding and computer science. If a student is interested, he or she can go on to more advanced coding lessons. By 2017, more than 300 million people worldwide had tried the Hour of Code.

Tim Cook, the head of computer company Apple, watches as kids participate in an Hour of Code event at an Apple Store.

People can access the Hour of Code at home, but each year, Code.org also hosts a worldwide Hour of Code event. The event takes place during the Computer Science Education Week at the beginning of December. Partners such as Disney, Apple, and Google help spread the word. In 2016, Disney made a new Hour of Code lesson based on the animated film *Moana*. Microsoft made several tutorials related to the popular game *Minecraft*. A group of athletes, including Kobe Bryant and Serena Williams, helped promote a sports-themed lesson. And in Apple Stores across the world, students could participate in a one-hour coding lesson.

These early coding lessons often use a concept called block coding. This means students don't have to jump straight

into writing code. Instead, they move blocks labeled with commands around the screen. These blocks may say "move forward" or "turn left." The character on the screen then follows the actions. This helps students understand the basic process of giving logical instructions to the computer. As the lessons progress, the challenges become more complex and more block commands are added. Eventually students begin writing actual code.

Learning to Code in School

In schools across the country, coding is becoming a common subject. Alongside math and social studies, kids are learning the basics of how to make computer programs. Most of these courses are in middle and high schools. The number of schools offering programming classes is expected to rise in the coming years.

Students also learn to code in after-school and summer programs. One of these is CS@SC Summer Camps, held at the University of Southern California. The weeklong camps are designed to give students from preschool to high school early exposure to coding, helping them think about how computers work in their daily lives. Students learn what computer science is and how programs are written. They also get a preview of what college life is like.

Learning how to program has advantages beyond preparing students for coding careers. It also teaches students to think like a programmer, which can improve their problem-solving skills in other areas. Coding can give students another set of critical thinking tools, especially when thinking about how to tackle big projects of all kinds.

Experts predict there will be a major demand for programmers in the future. Students who aren't exposed to

Learning the basics of coding in elementary school can give students a head start on their later programming education.

programming in high school may not have the chance to see if it is interesting to them. Giving students the chance to code early means that many more may choose to pursue computer science. This can help satisfy the future need for coders.

Coding for a Mobile Future

In the last decade, the popularity of mobile devices has boomed. Smartphones kicked off this wave, bringing amazing computing power into the palms of people's hands.

DID YOU KNOW?

Computers and coding have enabled a new type of acting in Hollywood movies. It is known as motion capture. An actor is covered with a bunch of white or green dots. Special sensors record how the dots move as the actor performs in a scene. The facial movements are then transferred to a digital character, such as an alien or a magical beast. The end result is similar to acting with a high-tech mask.

By the late 2010s, the hottest trend was wearable technology. Devices such as the FitBit or the Apple Watch are worn on the wrist. Some track fitness information, such as heart rate or running distance. Others can send messages or play music. The future is likely to bring devices that are even smaller and more capable. Imagine jewelry that is connected to a phone. A person could answer a call with a tap of an earring. Coding for these devices will require a lot of creative thinking. One of the biggest hurdles with wearable technology is battery life. Small devices can fit only small batteries. Smart, efficient programming can help these items run on less power, extending the battery life.

Coding for Virtual Spaces

Another field that will require creative coding is virtual reality. Virtual reality immerses the user in an entirely different world. A user puts on a headset and is transported to a virtual location. Small screens in front of the eyes create the illusion of being in a three-dimensional environment. Headphones produce noises that sound as if they are coming from specific directions. And when the user turns his or her head, the screens and headphones work together to match this movement in the virtual world.

In virtual reality, the user moves through a landscape and interacts with virtual objects. For example, with the headset on, a user may be exploring a house. When the user wants to open a door, he or she reaches out to grasp the

Virtual reality technology is making new kinds of computer experiences possible.

knob. Of course, the door isn't really there. Programmers have to create code that displays the door knob in the right location and causes it to turn when the user grasps it. In other words, the game must react to both what the user is seeing and what the user is doing.

Augmented reality has similar demands but works slightly different. While virtual reality involves worlds that are entirely created in a computer, augmented reality blends computer programming with the real world. One of the best examples is the mobile game *Pokémon GO*. The game took the world by storm in the summer of 2016. In *Pokémon GO*, the user sees a map of the surrounding area. Creatures appear in particular locations on the map. When the user taps a creature, the map goes away and the phone displays a view through the device's camera. A three-dimensional rendering of the creature appears on the screen, overlaid on the camera view. It looks as though

HoloLens: Bringing Augmented Reality into the Home

Computer company Microsoft created an augmented reality device called HoloLens. The HoloLens is a set of big glasses that a user can wear. Through the glasses, the user sees three-dimensional objects in his or her environment. Imagine a phone's screen floating in midair. You could click on the e-mail app and it would open, allowing you to write a message without using a keyboard. Microsoft also thinks the augmented reality technology could be used by artists. A sculptor could design a statue of a horse in a HoloLens app. That statue then could be created by a three-dimensional printer. The programming opportunities with HoloLens are huge, but they will require a lot of work. Since the HoloLens is meant to be used by everyday people, programmers will have a lot of users test their creations.

This promotional photo from Microsoft shows a motorcycle designer using HoloLens to view her creation on her desktop.

world. When archaeologists find ancient ruins, they may try to describe or sketch what the ruins might have once looked like. With an augmented reality program, they can see these recreations overlaid on the ruins themselves. Someone walking through ruins in Greece could hold up a phone or tablet and see how the place would have looked in 500 BCE.

Artificial Intelligence

One major area of study in programming today is artificial intelligence. In this field, coders work to create smart software that can solve problems and adapt to new situations on its own. Simple versions of artificial intelligence are responsible for the challenging computer opponents found in modern video games. These

the creature really exists in the user's environment.

However, coders are using augmented reality for more than creating games. Some have designed a new way to see an old

opponents are programmed to adapt to new situations created by the player's actions. For example, in a football game, the artificial intelligence might make adjustments to its team's defense based on the play style of the user. Making smarter robots is another application of artificial intelligence. Robotic vacuum cleaners learn how to clean a room, how to avoid obstacles, and when to return to their base to recharge their batteries. However, there are many other ways programmers are bringing smart technology to the world.

The computer Watson is one of the most famous artificial intelligence machines. It was built by the company IBM through years of hardware and software development. Watson competed on the quiz show *Jeopardy!* in 2011. It beat two human players. IBM later adapted Watson to use its intelligence in the field of health care. It analyzes a

Self-Modifying Code

What happens when a program becomes its own programmer? Though human programmers try to make software that can work perfectly, they can't anticipate every issue that may arise. Instead of the programmer having to go back in and rework the code, a self-modifying program could just rewrite its own code. The hope is that such smart software would be able to adapt itself to carry out complex tasks. For example, the US government hopes to make self-learning computers that can assess situations based on huge amounts of complex information. Computers can store vastly more data than human analysts. A smart, adaptable computer with access to all this information may be able to suggest the best decisions in high-stakes situations, such as natural disasters or wars.

wide variety of patient data, then makes recommendations to doctors. In 2016, IBM announced that Watson would begin working on weather forecasts as well.

Coding a New World

As computers and electronic devices become more sophisticated, coding will have to adapt as well. Programmers will continue developing innovative new software to run on these machines. From animated movies to virtual video games to weather forecasts, code has a nearly infinite number of uses in our digital future.

GLOSSARY

binary (BYE-nary): A number system that consists solely of ones and zeroes.

compiler (com-PIE-ler): A software program that translates code into a program that can run on a computer.

encryption (en-CRIP-shun): The process of turning information into a form that prevents it from being read.

operating systems (OP-er-ay-ting SIS-temz): The most basic software on a computer that helps the other software work together with the hardware.

processor (PRAW-sess-er): The part of the computer that carries out the instructions of programs.

smartphones (SMART-fonez): Cell phones that have a large touchscreen and a powerful processor and can run apps.

three-dimensional (three-duh-MENSH-un-uhl): Having height, width, and depth.

web browsers (WEB brow-zerz): Software programs that allow a user to access the World Wide Web, part of the Internet.

Books

Heather Lyons and Elizabeth Tweedale, *Learn to Program*. Minneapolis, MN: Lerner Publications, 2017. This book provides some basic information for beginning programmers, explaining concepts such as algorithms, loops, and variables.

Jon Woodcock, *Coding Games in Scratch: A Step-by-Step Visual Guide to Building Your Own Computer Games*. New York: DK, 2016. This guide for new programmers shows how to build programs with the Scratch programming language. Users can create puzzles, mazes, and other interactive games.

Sean McManus, *How to Code in 10 Easy Lessons: Learn How to Design and Code Your Very Own Computer Game*. Lake Forest, CA: Walter Foster Jr, 2015. This helpful guide breaks down ten key skills that new programmers should learn. Readers will be able to create games and web pages.

Tammy Gagne, *Women in Computer Science*. Minneapolis, MN: Abdo Publishing, 2017. This book includes examples of women doing incredible work in many areas of computer science, including coding.

Therese Naber, *How the Computer Changed History*. Minneapolis, MN: Abdo Publishing, 2016. In this book, discover the amazing story behind how computers went from expensive, room-sized machines to something that millions of people carry with them in their pockets every day.

Websites

Code Academy (https://www.codecademy.com/) The Code Academy website features free lessons on many different programming languages, including Python, Java, and Ruby.

Hour of Code (https://code.org/learn) The website for the Hour of Code has links to dozens of coding tutorials. Many of the tutorials feature popular characters, such as those from the Star Wars films and *Minecraft*.

Lightbot (https://lightbot.com/) On the Lightbot website, users can tackle puzzles using basic programming concepts, helping them to think like coders.

Made w/Code (https://www.madewithcode.com/) The Made w/Code site, run by technology company Google, features many fun and interesting coding projects.

Scratch (https://scratch.mit.edu/) The Massachusetts Institute of Technology (MIT) runs this coding site, which uses an easy-to-learn programming language called Scratch to introduce users to coding concepts.

INDEX

A
Analytical Engine, 8
Apple, 11, 33, 36
Apps, 13, 18, 20, 23, 30, 39
Artificial intelligence, 40–42
Augmented reality, 38–40

B
Babbage, Charles, 7–8
Big data, 25–26, 27
Binary, 15–16
Bryant, Kobe, 33
Bugs, 17–18

C
Coding
    bootcamp, 30
    in schools, 34–35
Compiler, 16
Computers
    hardware, 14, 18, 41
    software, 14–15, 16–17, 18,
        23–24, 40

D
Data centers, 27
Difference Engine, 7, 8

E
E-mail, 12, 22, 39
Encryption, 22–24
Errors, 16–18
    runtime error, 17
    syntax error, 16–17

F
Facebook, 26, 27
Fitness devices, 36

G
Games, 4, 10, 15, 18, 20, 28–30, 33,
    38, 40–42
Google, 33

H
Hackers, 24–25
"Hello World" programs, 6
Hopper, Grace, 9, 17
Hour of Code, 31–33
HTML, 19

I
IBM, 10, 11, 41–42
Internet, 10, 12–13

L
Linux, 21
Lord Byron, 7
Lovelace, Ada, 6–9

M
Malware, 24–25
Marconi, Guglielmo, 25
Menabrea, Luigi Federico, 8
Microsoft HoloLens, 39
Microsoft Windows XP, 17
Minecraft (game), 33

Motion capture, 36
Movies, 26–28, 36

N
National STEM Video Game
    Challenge, 20

O
Operating systems, 17, 21

P
Personal computers, 10–11
Petrov, Stanlislaus, 18
Pokémon GO (game), 38
Programming languages, 6
  C#, 15
  COBOL, 9
  FORTRAN, 10
  Java, 6, 15
  JavaScript, 19
  Python, 15
  Swift, 15
Purdue University, 15

R
Robots, 27, 40, 41

S
Self-modifying code, 42
Smartphones, 13, 35
Social networks, 25–26

T
Tablets, 13, 40
Telegraph, 25
Thinking like a programmer,
    18–21
Three-dimensional computer
    graphics, 27–29
Torvalds, Linus, 21
Toy Story (film), 28

U
UNIVAC I, 9

V
Virtual reality, 37, 38
Viruses, 24–25

W
Watson (computer), 41–42
Web browsers, 15, 19
Westworld (film), 27
Williams, Serena, 33
World War II, 9, 10
World Wide Web, 12–13, 19

Z
Z3, 9
Zuse, Konrad, 9, 10

Meg Marquardt started as a scientist but decided she liked writing about science even more. She enjoys researching physics, geology, and climate science. She lives in Madison, Wisconsin, with her two scientist cats, Lagrange and Doppler.